Depression:
A Survivor's Guide

ROLAND HOLCOMBE

Depression: A Survivor's Guide

Copyright © 2017 Roland K. Holcombe

Unless otherwise indicated, all scripture quotations are taken from the New King James Version ®, Copyright © 1982 by Thomas Nelson Inc. Used by permission. All rights reserved.

ISBN-10: 0-9987696-0-6

ISBN-13: 978-0-9987696-0-8

First Edition

Cover Design and Layout by Michael R. Carter

All rights reserved under International Copyright Law. Contents and/or cover may not be reproduced in whole or in part in any form without the expressed written consent of the Publisher.

Published By:

Single Eye Press
P.O. Box 2785
Gadsden AL 35903

SingleEyePress@mail.com
www.rolandholcombe.net

Dedication

To all those who feel lost and unloved

and have not yet been set free

Contents

Introduction
–9–

Ch. 1: There is Hope
–12–

Ch. 2: A Brief Look at My own Story
–19–

**Ch. 3: To Understand Depression:
More About Perspective**
–22–

Ch. 4: The Importance of Understanding Our identity
–25–

**Ch. 5: The History of Psychology:
A Way That Seems Right to a Man**
–28–

Ch. 6: Causes of Depression
–35–

Ch. 7: Typical Treatment for Depression
–39–

Ch. 8: A Practical Approach
–43–

Ch. 9: Understanding God and Myself
–47–

Ch. 10: The Spiritual Roots of Depression
–53–

Ch. 11: Know Who You Are and How to Fight
–61–

Ch. 12: The Past: Let it Go
–69–

Ch. 13: The Potential Pitfall and Problems of Therapy and Treatment
–72–

Ch. 14: Make Your List: Divine Cognitive Therapy
–76–

Ch.15: Depression in the Bible
–80–

Ch. 16: Fear and Loneliness
–85–

Ch. 17: The Wrap Up
–90–

Appendix A
–93–

Appendix B
–97–

Abstract
–100–

"I call heaven and earth as witnesses today against you, that I have set before you life and death, blessing and cursing; therefore choose life, that both you and your descendants may live; that you may love the LORD your God, that you may obey His voice, and that you may cling to Him, for He is your life and the length of your days;"

Deuteronomy 30: 19-20

Introduction

It's About Perspective

Depression sucks. It is a cunning and deceitful ailment that sabotages any attempt to address it. As a clinician providing treatment for depression, I have witnessed the struggle firsthand when those suffering do all they can to make it to an appointment and once there, don't have anything to say. The days seem endless and everything runs together. Sometimes you can't sleep at night and other times you want to sleep around the clock. Nobody gets it and you just don't have the energy to explain it one more time, so you quit answering the phone.

When I was desperate to crawl out of my own depression and my techniques had fallen flat, I recognized the root of this problem was much deeper than brain chemistry and behavior. I needed more than a pill that would start working in two to three weeks and a one-hour talk with someone. Have you suspected there may be a better way to deal with all of this? Have you asked yourself if there's something you have missed?

If you are willing to look in the places most don't want to—if you are willing to ask yourself the questions most of us stopped asking long ago—and if what you have been doing has not worked, you may be ready to receive what the Father has for those that are "the poor in spirit" like I was.

Sometimes you know when you are depressed. It is clear to you. You feel different but you're not sure why. You have lost interest in things you used to care about. Some begin to sleep longer and feel tired all the time. Others might not be able to sleep at all. It can be a feeling of just not quite being able to get it together and not having the energy to fight or care anymore. Depression may lead one to feel angry or irritable all the time but have no source for the anger. Are you depressed? Do you have the blues? Does characterizing depression as "the blues" seem ridiculous in comparison to the state you currently find yourself in?

Depression is a normal part of life. Most people will experience it sometime in their lifetime either in reaction to a life event or on its own. The following statement is my own and not meant to oversimplify. "It is our body and mind's response to something we are not getting that we need (love, fellowship, nutrition, exercise, relationship with God) or a by-product of something in our life that shouldn't be there (relationship, drugs or alcohol, habitual behaviors, resentment)."

Depression may come from an organic source (physical—due to medical reasons such as disease or injury) or inorganic (behavior/emotion/spiritual—due to a bad habits, grief or loss of a close friend/relative, break-up of a relationship, or significant life events). This book is intended to point you in the direction of healing and, in no way, render any type of medical advice. I am not a physician. I do know a lot about depression and depressive illness and its treatment. I have made it a point of study for several years because I battled it in my own life and am an overcomer.

If you put into practice the suggestions that follow, you will get better and it will be helpful for your recovery. Is this a cure all for depression? No. If you are depressed due to being diabetic and are unable to regulate your insulin levels thus causing chemical imbalance, go see a doctor. If you also experience anger and resentment due to abuse as a child and have unforgiveness towards people in your past, keep reading. You are on the right track.

It is important to understand why you are depressed. It is important to know the source of your depression to determine how best to approach treatment. It is helpful to be able to gauge the severity, when it began, and how long has it been going on. It is also necessary to know to what extent it is impairing your ability to function.

1

There is Hope

Jesus said: "Come to Me, all you who are weary and heavy laden, and I will give you rest.

"Take My yoke upon you and learn from Me, for I am gentle and humble in heart, and you will find rest for your souls.

"For My yoke is easy and My burden light" (Matthew 11:28-30 NASB).

There may not ever be a time in your life when you feel as "weary" or "heavy laden" as you or someone you love does now. This heaviness seems to have a literal weight that can be crushing yet we give it a non-threatening name like "depression." If you've never heard those words above, they might have shed a little light of hope into your mind. They are the words of Jesus, who created us.

There is Hope

You are probably looking at this book because you or someone close to you struggles with depression. Your interest is more than intellectual curiosity. My own battle with depression stretched far longer than I would have believed possible. I know the misery of not wanting to exist but too tired to consider ending my own life. I have walked alone in the shadowy areas of life without hope. I have felt my own life was a burden, hating each moment that ticked away, believing there was nothing to look forward to. My past was too painful to touch or to think about. I have spent hours crying out to God to end my life or take away the pain I was feeling. I did all this immersed in Christian culture hanging on for some reprieve while those around me seemed to wonder what I'd done to bring this on myself. This book is my lifeline to you, my brothers and sisters.

There is a vibrant, joy-full life right at your fingertips unlike any you've ever considered. Despite the misery depression brings, it can be a positive agent if it has gotten your attention, making you stop and examine life thoroughly. If you are a believing Christian, you are no longer "seated" in this world. That's why you feel so out of place here. You were created in the image of God specifically for His purpose. You were born into a time and place where there is an ongoing, continuous battle in a dimension that is not visible to most. In fact, most people around you don't even know there is a battle going on. They are getting slaughtered before they ever enter the battle. Your enemy is cunning. He is trying to distract or lure you to sleep so you never become a threat to him. He roams about seeking to sabotage you so you never realize your created value or potential.

If you are not a believer the enemy will still attack you, but it will be different. He will try to prevent you from ever learning how much your Father truly loves you. You might have more prejudice built up against listening to a message from someone who professes to know Christ. The teaching of the world aims to create doubt that you can ever really know anything. It paints those who profess an assurance as foolish.

Any battle is going to have bases of operation for each side and this is no different. For believers, that base on this earth is the church. The church consists of people who believe but have come to be represented by a building housing a corporation. Many of these bases are compromised by ineffective training of the "troops" and even by enemy agents. They seem non-threatening on the surface. The Bible calls them wolves dressed as sheep or false prophets. They have stopped teaching their soldiers about the battle or even that they're supposed to fight. They think we've already won and are waiting to claim the prize when the Master returns. Jesus has already won the victory, but we remain in the thick of battle as long as we are clothed in flesh. Many of these "double agents" have been lured into complacency by the enemy. They have grown comfortable, thinking their kingdom impenetrable. A good intelligence report would reveal to them their positions have already been overrun.

What you are feeling in your mind, your emotions, and throughout your body is the result of being beaten down, hit, defeated, and humiliated by a vicious enemy that prowls about like a roaring lion seeking to devour his prey. It is an enemy that has been kicking your butt for a long time and you don't stand a chance. You were never taught who you really were and what your life was meant to be about.

Imagine wandering onto a battlefield some sunny day, thinking you'd just go for a walk in the park. When you see a hostile

force bearing down on your position you freeze, retreat, or even ignore it like it's not there. You're just out for a walk in the park. The hostile force is on a mission to destroy any life in a certain sector or area. He will do anything it takes to accomplish this. He will use any means at his disposal to lure, trick, ambush, sabotage, deceive, or murder you. He will enlist other people you care about. He will co-opt those you trust in his operations and turn them against you. You still think you're walking in the park and you're getting used to the hostile force being around. You are even close to being able to ignore him. He wants you dead and almost has you. If your only context from experience is "this means I am taking a walk in the park" yet he is going all out to try and kill you, the disadvantage belongs to you. You are without defense for this battle. Wake up!

I am sounding an alarm in this book. It is a call for you to stand up and take notice. Wake up! He's almost gotten you and you never even began to fight. You were meant to have victory. You were meant to overcome. You are royalty and meant to inherit a kingdom unlike anything you'd ever imagined. Stand up, soldier, and hear these words. Stand up sons and daughters. This enemy knows you can crush him but he has you deceived. He tries to get you believing this is all there is. He can literally impact the chemicals in your brain and body to cause this depression, or "spirit of death," to linger about you. He whispers evil words of death into your mind. Are you willing to let light shine into your darkness? This can all change, beginning right now.

> *Father, I pray that light would shine into darkness that the enemy has created around the one reading these words. I ask You, in the name of Jesus, to make Yourself known to this person. I ask You to give them eyes to see and ears to hear. Amen.*

If you are not a Christian or believer, the prayer that follows is one to commit your life to Christ. It is to acknowledge Jesus as the Son of God and that He paid for your sins on the cross. You are saying that you need a savior and without Jesus you will be eternally separated from God. This is not a step to be taken lightly. You are saying you want to reconcile the relationship with your Father through Jesus Christ. If you're not ready, skip it for now. Read the book and see if it rings true. At the end, you can pull it back up. If God has spoken to you, give your life to Him.

If you are a believer, the prayer is to repent of current sins and rebellion in your life. The prayer is your return to your Father. Begin seeking that relationship for which you were made. It is a rebirth or a renewal.

Pray the following prayer aloud before continuing. It is an important part of this process:

> *Father, I believe You sent Jesus to die for my sins and make a way for me to get back to You. I believe and accept His sacrifice for me, and know His shed blood cleanses me from all unrighteousness. I repent of my sins. I ask forgiveness for: (call out specific sins brought to your mind by the Holy Spirit). I give up my life to be hidden in You. May the Holy Spirit apply the blood of Jesus to my past, my present, and my future. I believe I am made whole and healed by Your work on the cross, Jesus. I renounce a spirit of death and despair in the name of Jesus. I renounce a spirit of depression and fear. Father, please give me Your Holy Spirit—to dwell within me and seal me. Teach me about who I am*

*and what my purpose is. Thank You and I love You.
I pray this in the name of Your Son, Jesus. Amen.*

If you or someone you know has struggled with depression, what follows are practical but simple suggestions to help you get better. Through psychology you may find empathy and some short-term relief. Through Christ you can be healed. Through Christ you can be set free!

> Be sober, be vigilant; because your adversary the devil walks about like a roaring lion, seeking whom he may devour (I Peter 5:8 NKJV).

> Then Jesus said to those Jews who believed Him, "If you abide in My word, you are my disciples indeed. "And you shall know the truth, and the truth shall make you free" (John 8:31-32 NKJV).

> A Song at the dedication of the house of David. I will extol You, O LORD, for You have lifted me up, and have not let my foes rejoice over me.
> O LORD my God, I cried out to You, and You healed me.
> O LORD, You brought my soul up from the grave; You have kept me alive, that I should not go down to the pit.   Sing praise to the LORD, you saints of His, And give thanks to the remembrance of His holy name.
> For His anger is but for a moment, His

favor is for life; Weeping may endure for a night, but joy comes in the morning (Psalm 30:1-5 NKJV).

2

A Brief Look at My Own Story

When I was in college at a small Christian school in Nashville, TN, I had my first experience with what was diagnosed as Major Depressive Disorder. As I looked back on that time, it wasn't truly my first experience. I had depression intruding into my life as early as age seventeen in response to some real-life events but didn't label it depression. As a teen, I had to go to school like every other kid and just kind of floated along because I was smart. During adulthood when I had all these commitments to work, school, friends, and ministry it became noticeable. People in my life began to ask what was wrong.

Things changed quickly for me. I went from carrying a full load of classes, working part-time split with duties as a resident assistant, representative in student government, and campus ministry leader, as well as maintaining a very active social life to not wanting or feeling like getting out of bed. It happened practically overnight. Looking back, I believe it was triggered in part by a difficult relationship I was in at the time. It hit me out of nowhere. My legs were cut out from under me. I simply didn't care about life or movement or anything anymore.

My faith seemed distant and belonging to someone else. I initially avoided friends, didn't answer calls, and went out only at night to get food when nobody else was likely to notice me. I missed chapel, which was required three times a week to stay enrolled in college. I didn't do the room checks required of me as a resident assistant. I quit going to classes. I felt like everyone was staring at me and seeing something was wrong. My friends began to keep their distance as if I might have something contagious.

There are things or feelings that I remember from this time period that really stand out even now. I remember this profound sense of loneliness and isolation, even in the middle of a college dormitory with friends living all around me. There was this sense of self-consciousness about everything that I'd never felt before. I was a confident and cocky guy before it hit and now I wanted to keep my eyes downcast to pretend that nobody was seeing me. I felt like everything was in slow motion, and I badly wanted to disappear.

I eventually went to the dean over student life to tell her I couldn't seem to function anymore. She suggested I see one of the professors in the psychology department. I made an appointment and was quickly seen for counseling. After hearing my symptoms and talking about what was bothering me, he referred me to a psychiatrist. I made an appointment and saw him maybe ten days later. I was diagnosed with major depression and given a prescription for an anti-depressant called Prozac. The doctor suggested I withdraw from my classes and responsibilities for the time being and see a therapist. I followed his suggestion and spent the remainder of that semester sleeping and going to weekly therapy appointments. After a few months I began to get better and, at least, regained some desire to participate in life. However, I never felt quite the same after getting hit with that first bout of depression. It seemed like a monster that was constantly lurking over my shoulder waiting to hit me when I least expected. It was a monster I would become well acquainted with over the next several years.

3

To Understand Depression: More About Perspective

If you discuss the bulk of our understanding on depression (what an average person will believe about it), our knowledge is based in science and what I will call "the wisdom of man." Information is frequently pushed by the pharmaceutical companies to educate people they believe might benefit from their new drug. That is often in opposition to a spiritual perspective on depression, although most of us aren't aware of it. We must look at the whole picture to see clearly in order to get out of the hole we find ourselves in. Whatever perspective we adopt in understanding depression will completely determine how it is treated and if that treatment will be successful. In this book, the spiritual perspective is only considered as originating from God's Word, the Bible.

To Understand Depression: More About Perspective

What we understand depression to be is important when it comes to the restoration of mental and emotional health. Whether you are a Christian or not, your understanding of depression has been filtered through the lens of modern science. Those who treat depression such as medical doctors, psychiatrists, therapists, and psychologists have been trained from a perspective that man is nothing more than an accidental evolved animal who happens to be fortunate enough to have gained consciousness after millions of years. They may not even know or realize that this is the foundation underpinning the techniques and means of treatment. There are some exceptions out there facilitated by Christians who understand this, but they are rare.

The fields of study that address depression are psychology, psychiatry, and social sciences. They are the exercise of man's collected wisdom to explain who man really is without acknowledging God as his creator. All scientific theory related to human growth and development, anatomy and physiology, neuropsychology, neurology, biology, psychology, etc. is missing the foundational bedrock that man was created in the image of God for His purpose. The ideas and understanding of who we are as created beings is absent from medical science and all the following layers of academic study, theories of personality, and attempts to treat various manifestations of this absence known as mental illness. The textbook term for mental illness is psychopathology.

Often, because of unbelief and closed minds, many who attempt to provide healing to the hurting individual with depression are operating in the dark. There are plenty of well-meaning individuals that hone their technique and some even are believers in Christ. As with most professionals, they are trained by our universities to keep faith compartmentalized, rarely crossing into practice when in a professional setting.

Because of the radically different belief system of those who treat depression from an evolutionary "we're just high functioning animals" perspective, the treatment will have a radically different focus. We are taught in our schools and universities to separate issues of faith from science and the practice of medicine or psychology. It is the spirit man in us that makes us who we are. Ignorance of this truth creates an ineffective response from providers who don't understand and add more frustration to the suffering. It is like cartoons operating in a 2 dimensional world trying to have an impact on 3 and 4 dimensional objects. They might as well be veterinarians for all they understand man to be.

4

The Importance of Understanding Our Identity

This may just blow you away if you've never heard this. This is an extremely important, life altering, make it or break it concept you must get! Men and women, all of us, are eternal spiritual beings created in the image of God for His purpose. That purpose is to walk and talk with Him in intimacy as Adam and Eve did in the Garden of Eden. Those who haven't heard the Gospel and believed, been baptized, and received the Holy Spirit are separated from God, their Creator. The purpose of our existence is to reconcile with our Father and in turn become a "minister of reconciliation" or "ambassador" in representing Him. This only happens by the work of Jesus on the cross.

> Then God said, "Let Us make man in
> Our image, according to Our likeness; let them

have dominion over the fish of the sea, over the birds of the air, and over the cattle, over all the earth and over every creeping thing that creeps upon the earth" (Genesis 1:26 NKJV).

For we are His workmanship, created in Christ Jesus for good works, which God prepared beforehand that we should walk in them (Ephesians 2:10 NKJV).

Now all things are of God, who has reconciled us to Himself through Jesus Christ, and has given us the ministry of reconciliation (II Corinthians 5:18 NKJV).

In this is love, not that we loved God, but that He loved us and sent His Son to be the propitiation for our sins (I John 4:10 NKJV).

And we have known and believed the love that God has for us. God is love, and he who abides in love abides in God, and God in him (I John 4:16 NKJV).

If you claim to be a Christian (believer): Many of us had a big emotional moment in church long ago, but when it was all over we weren't quite sure what we believed in except Jesus being the Son of God and dying for us on the cross. We were never taught who we really were if we believed and professed Christ. Were you ever really taught that you should spend time learning what it means to be a Christian or follower of Christ? When you believed, did you know fully what it meant? I was in a Christian college and in the midst of a great identity crisis and didn't even know it. How could I have missed this with all my exposure to church? Where and who were the real Christians?

The question had to be asked, "I go to church, why haven't I heard about this before?" The sad truth is that most churches are run and governed by people who don't know who they are or what they are supposed to be about. They have become institutions that only focus on keeping the institution going. They don't have faith, so they have resorted to adopting the same ways of dealing with problems and life's difficulties as the world. When a person doesn't know who they are, it is called an identity crisis. "Who am I?" This is one of the first big philosophical questions we ask ourselves throughout our childhood and adolescence to find our identity. Most of us will also ask, "Who am I in relation to God?" Many people wander into a church during an exploratory or tumultuous period only to wander back out, yet they still cling to their identification as a Christian.

Trying to make it in the world on what most churches teach you about being a Christian resembles someone trying to survive by eating only stale, out-of-date Flintstone vitamins for years. There might be some occasional nutritional value in it, but it's manufactured and certainly won't keep your whole body alive spiritually.

Christianity, faith, and walking like Jesus did are not things that can be manufactured by applying "a little bit of this or a little bit of that." It is a living, supernatural existence that flows out of intimacy with our Heavenly Father, the indwelling Holy Spirit, and being transformed by the Word of God.

5

The History of Psychology: A Way That Seems Right to a Man

I'm going to take some liberties here when discussing psychology and lump it in with psychiatry because there was little difference when it began. We are discussing the science of human behavior (and animal behavior). People of faith sometimes can't comprehend the way those without faith believe. They make assumptions about others never realizing how vastly different their perspectives are. Without Christ, everyone is literally blind and deaf when approaching anything related to other created beings. They will sometimes stumble onto some truth but what they miss will likely be huge. Let me give you an example from the history of psychology.

Founded in Reason, Logic, and Atheism

The Greeks, where much of psychological theory originated, believed in many gods but were not acquainted with the only

God. They moved away from belief in the supernatural towards reason, logic, and naturalism in explaining man. All modern psychology traces its roots back to either Sigmund Freud or B.F. Skinner. These men influenced all the other major players; therefore, I won't discuss them all. Freud theorized that we were split into three compartments, the id, the ego, and the superego. The id was primitive, the ego had basic functioning to govern, and the superego was where consciousness resided. He considered religion to be more of an illness and termed it neuroses. In one of his final works, "The Future of an Illusion," Freud spoke of religion as an illusion of "wish fulfillment" and a primitive attempt to make us feel safe with an imaginary father figure. Freud was not capable of understanding man as he is described in the following Scriptures:

> **Just as it is written: "God has given them a spirit of stupor, eyes that they should not see and ears that they should not hear, to this very day.**
> **And David says: "Let their table become a snare and a trap, a stumbling block and a recompense to them.**
> **Let their eyes be darkened, so that they do not see, and bow down their back always (Romans 11:8-10 NKJV).**

B.F. Skinner, who is the founder of behavioral psychology, saw man as an animal and implied that he had no free will or consciousness. He believed behaviors were learned and conditioned by our environment and reinforcement, social interaction, as well as our genetic makeup. All our approaches to the treatment of illnesses like depression evolved from variations of Freud and Skinner's theories. Much of our society's structure and systems are based on Skinner's principles of behavioral psychology. If your basis for understanding man is founded on ideas from these two veins of thought, any approach to restoration will only be by accident. It will not address more than the surface level or shallow difficulties faced. They won't touch the source or root of illness.

Why This is Important to Know

Legally, if I were going to do an experiment on you, I would have to do what is called "Informed Consent." This is a legal and ethical imperative to let someone know the risks and potential consequences of engaging in whatever it is I am promoting. I am providing a "full disclosure" here because I have studied it and come to understand the value in knowing what you are getting up front. If the fields of psychology and psychiatry do not acknowledge the existence of God or that our created purpose is to have an intimate relationship with Him, they will never get the answer right to the question being asked. Depression is serious, particularly when you acknowledge that some depressed people kill themselves. If you have had serious depression that hasn't resolved itself, then you really need to know this information. The practitioners of this field don't even know they don't know the answer to your questions of "What's happening to me and how do I get better?" I spent years going to these guys for answers about why I felt like I did and how to deal with it. When I learned the truth, within a few weeks my depression was gone—removed never to return. I was set free.

It is not the purpose of this book to argue about Scripture or belief systems. I will give specific Scripture verses to show how it addresses what I am saying for each point. If you are hurting and suffering from depression, then hear this truth I am speaking.

You have a Father in heaven that loves you and wants to talk with you every day. You may not have ever been told this or it may have been misrepresented by people who didn't really represent Him in the way they lived their lives. If you don't open your eyes to this truth and listen, your life will continue to be wrecked because your spirit is crying out for intimacy with Him and you are avoiding it.

If hearing my appeal to introduce Scripture and mention God makes you angry or tempts you to turn away, consider not only what I am saying but what my qualifications are for saying it. I was depressed for many years and was healed. If God will do that for me, why wouldn't He also do it for you? This works and will change your life.

> For though we walk in the flesh, we do not war according to the flesh.
> For the weapons of our warfare are not carnal but mighty in God for pulling down strongholds,
> casting down arguments and every high thing that exalts itself against the knowledge of God, bringing every thought into captivity to the obedience of Christ (II Corinthians 10:3-5 NKJV).
>
> We are of God. He who knows God hears us; he who is not of God does not hear us. By this we know the spirit of truth and the spirit of error (I John 4:6 NKJV).
>
> To the law and to the testimony! If they do not speak according to His word, it is because there is no light in them (Isaiah 8:20 NKJV).

How Receiving Treatment Without Meeting God Will Impact You

The understanding of the modern psychiatrist, through the lens of the medical model, behavioral theory, and psychodynamic training is going to direct their focus on diagnosing you according to a checklist for insurance purposes (and their own liability insurance). They will focus on the immediate symptoms—insomnia, fatigue, anxiety, isolation, etc. and then prescribe medication to chemically counter what your body is doing. There is little concern for why you may truly be depressed.

It is unlikely they'll be able to spend enough time with you or ask that you have a complete physical to rule out medical causes even though they know that is the best practice. You may be referred to a therapist or psychologist if the depression is severe enough. They will focus on the problem—depression—and address any negative thoughts—"I am worthless, I am ugly, I will always fail," possibly getting you to counter with positive things—"I have worth, I am handsome, I will succeed." Their goal is to get you to feel better with the right mix of chemistry and simple exercises so you return to functioning. From a life perspective of understanding we are eternal beings, this is like preparing someone who is going on a walking trip around the world by repeatedly telling them how to tie their shoes. It might even go as deep as to suggest a different brand of shoe, but it will never address the journey, the importance of being ready to go at the right time, and being fit enough to complete the task. What follows is the checklist for a diagnosis of Major Depressive Disorder.

Criteria for Diagnosis of Depression

If you are experiencing the following things in your life, you could qualify for a medical diagnosis of depression called Major Depressive Disorder. There are some things a professional will look for, and the determination will be based on questions you answer about yourself. A person must have experienced the symptoms for more than two weeks.

- A depressed mood characterized by feeling sad, empty, or hopeless that lasts most of the day, every day for more than two weeks.
- No interest in normal activities or pleasure most of the day every day.
- Weight loss or weight gain.
- Difficulty sleeping—can't fall asleep or wake up frequently or sleeping all the time.
- Psychomotor agitation or retardation every day. This means you can't relax or rest and are moving constantly, or moving slowly, or not at all.
- Feeling fatigued, as if you have no energy daily.
- Feeling that you are worthless or having excessive/inappropriate guilt every day.
- Having more difficulty thinking or concentrating and/or indecisiveness daily than is normal for you.
- Recurrent thoughts of death, suicidal ideation with no plan, a suicide attempt, or a plan to commit suicide.

These symptoms must cause you significant distress and impair you functioning at your job, home, school, etc. For a diagnosis of depression, it cannot be due to a medical condition or the effects of a substance. It is not paired with more debilitating symptoms like hallucinations or delusions that would generate another diagnosis.

The psychiatrist that will make the determination if someone meets the criteria for Major Depressive Disorder will also ask questions to rule out mania. This is a symptom that goes with another illness or type of depression and involves agitation, increased goal directed behavior, euphoria, grandiosity, and the reduced need for sleep, to name a few.

6

Causes of Depression

Medical Reasons People Get Depressed

Following surgery of any kind or after having anesthesia—Many who experience major surgeries such as coronary bypass, removal of tumors or organs, repair of joints, tendons, etc. will experience reactive depression resulting from being put to sleep. I am not sure why this happens, but it does and competent physicians will warn you of this ahead of time. It will be listed as a potential side affect on the sheet you sign giving consent for treatment.

Following a head injury of any type—A severe head injury can lead to depression for years following the time the injury was received (Holsinger, T.). A traumatic brain injury varies in the level of severity. It can be mild, moderate, or severe.

A mild concussion has been associated with an increased risk of depression. More severe head injuries have been associated with the development or increased risk of developing schizophrenia, bipolar disorder, and depression.

After experiencing a Stroke or CVA—After someone experiences a stroke or cerebrovascular accident it is common for him or her to experience depression (Jorgensen, TS). A CVA is similar to a head injury in its destruction of brain cells. The injury is caused by deprivation of oxygen or blockage of blood flow. The risk is greater in the first three months following the stroke.

Secondary to another medical condition—or as a side effect of medication used to treat another condition: Any illness or disease that impacts your neurochemistry, hormone levels, or major system of the body can cause disruption and lead to depression. Some typical examples are: diabetes, menopause, andropause, cancer, thyroid disease, Parkinson's disease, Multiple Sclerosis, etc. Contributors to depression can either be the disease itself disrupting functioning or an emotional response to a reduction in the ability to function (grieving). Many medications used to treat illnesses have a possible side effect of depression.

Non-Medical Reasons People Get Depressed

Secondary to another mental health condition—Depression can be a by-product of any type of substance abuse disorder. The use of alcohol or other drugs leads to depression. Many times, anxiety that impairs functioning can lead to the development of depression. Post-Traumatic Stress Disorder also has high co-morbidity (likely to have both at the same time) rates with depression.

Due to Life Changes—Many life changes involve loss or grief. Grief sometimes leads to depression. A diagnosis of depression is based on the severity and duration of depressive symptoms. A treatment provider will also consider the degree of impairment. Some typical circumstances that can lead to depression: Death of a family member or close friend, loss of job, adjusting to illness or disease, financial distress, being in an accident, becoming the victim of a crime, or any life event that significantly increases stress levels.

As a Direct Consequence of One's Poor Decisions—Sometimes we do foolish things that lead to depression—marrying the alcoholic girlfriend to save her, having an abortion in high school, playing the lottery as a bill paying strategy, trying IV drug use and contracting hepatitis are examples of this. Many of us never were taught the right way to do things. Most of us are in relationships that were influenced by what we did or didn't see in our parents. Right now, no matter what you've done or where you've been, you can begin to live a different life. You can be transformed by God and make decisions being led by the Holy Spirit. Establish your identity by who God says you are, not by what the world has said about you. Forget the past that lies behind and look forward to what lies ahead.

Poor Stress Management—Stress is a heightened state of arousal in our body in response to prolonged stimulation. Life events or changes, as mentioned above, can contribute to heightened stress even if they are positive. At times, increased stress is unavoidable and completely normal. It helps us to have energy and drive to complete the increased demands placed on us in that moment. A healthy mind and body will return to a balanced state. Some will have difficulty regulating the stress response and will maintain the heightened state of stress for more prolonged time periods. Life events such as the death of a friend or family member, financial loss, or a disabling injury will naturally impact one for a longer time. Much of the stress response is determined by how we view our own circumstances and what we believe the outcome of current problems will be. From the spiritual perspective to reduce stress, think again, "Cast your burdens on Jesus for He cares for you" and "Come unto Me all ye who are weary and heavy laden and I will give you rest."

7

Typical Treatment For Depression

When one gets miserable enough they will seek help. If your depression is very severe or noticeable, it might be your friends or family members who urge you to seek treatment. People around you will notice when you are different. Nobody likes to be around someone who is depressed all the time. One of the typical characteristics of a depressed individual is that their focus turns inward on themselves. If you become apathetic about work or don't care enough to go, your survival becomes threatened. If you don't work, you can't pay your bills. If you have children to care for, they are dependent on you for their survival. You don't have an option to lie in bed or avoid work.

The Primary Care Physician: The first person most people will talk with about possibly being depressed is their family doctor.

The physician will often ask some diagnostic questions to gauge the severity of the problem. He may or may not want to conduct a thorough physical. Depending on your symptoms, the doctor will usually prescribe an anti-depressant medication for a short period of time. In rural areas, PCP's are sometimes the only ones available to prescribe anti-depressant medications. He may suggest that in addition to the medication you see a therapist.

Pastoral Counseling: If you attend church, a pastor might be the first person you'd consider talking with about your depression. Many pastors provide counseling in varying degrees and it will generally have a more spiritual focus involving Scripture. The counseling will often be free when done with your pastor.

Individual Therapy: Therapists meet with you for an hour each visit to talk about what might be bothering you, develop a plan for dealing with whatever the problem is, and helping you stay accountable to that plan. There are many types of clinicians who practice therapy: Social Workers, Counselors, Psychologists, and Marriage & Family Therapists. They will talk with you, listen to you, and help you discover why you may be depressed. They will also monitor you for potential safety issues and regularly ask you if you are having any suicidal thoughts. If you are currently experiencing any suicidal thoughts, call someone NOW or go to the nearest Emergency Department.

Grief Counseling: This is usually done by a therapist from the list above but focuses specifically on loss of loved ones and how to cope.

Psychiatry: This is the next step for those suffering beyond the primary care doctor. Many PCP's will refer to a psychiatrist because they specialize in prescribing psychotropic medication.

The psychiatrist will have an initial session to evaluate and diagnose, then will prescribe medication based on the severity of illness. The follow up sessions after the initial evaluation will usually be for only fifteen minutes to monitor medication.

Medication Management: Unfortunately, this is usually the first thing considered when people seek help for depression. Almost everyone has people in their family right now that are taking anti-depressants. A typical anti-depressant medication will not take effect for ten to fourteen days. Most research on anti-depressant medication is based on six weeks to ninety-day periods of treatment. They are initially marketed for "short-term relief" of depressive symptoms. What you are not told is that many people are encouraged to continue taking the anti-depressant medication to "ward off" the depression. Three months stretches out to twelve, then eighteen, with many taking the medications from that point onward. The newer medications in a class called SSRI's or blends of those drugs all have withdrawal effects. Some have serious withdrawal effects such as flu-like symptoms, muscle aches, sweating, temperature sensitivity, and anxiety for six to eight weeks or longer. Every physician I have heard discuss this minimizes the withdrawal impact, but I don't believe they have taken what they prescribe. Many people never get off these medications once they begin. Most of us don't have that kind of time to be "out of action" due to being sick from medication withdrawal. The withdrawal effects are alleviated if one tapers the medication (reduces the dosage) under a doctor's supervision over a three to six month period. Some will still have side effects. If you are truly struggling with thoughts of ending your life due to recurring depression, then the benefit is obviously worth the cost.

These medications also come with side effects, so be prepared. They may cause fatigue, depression, anxiety, insomnia, stomach upset, dry mouth, suicidal thinking and behavior, psychosis, and sexual impairment (difficulty with arousal, difficulty with ejaculation, decreased libido, hyper-sexuality).

8

A Practical Approach

Take action, no matter how small the beginning. Take one step towards dealing with your depression every day, no exceptions. "How do you walk 1,000 miles? One step at a time." "How do you eat an elephant? One bite at a time."

The following suggestions are simple life changes guaranteed to elevate your mood and decrease depressive symptoms.

There are some basic things a person can do that have been proven consistently to decrease depressive symptoms. The difficulty in implementing any of these comes when your depression has reached a point where you don't have the energy or motivation to try something different. If you can summon the ability to make yourself do some of these, despite how you feel, your depression should improve.

Take a walk once a day for ten to fifteen minutes. Any increase in activity will trigger your body to produce endorphins and more serotonin, which is a neurotransmitter that plays a huge role in mood.

Sit, stand, or do anything outside in the sunlight for at least thirty minutes a day. Sunlight triggers natural chemicals in the body to work that lead to improved mood.

Spend time with other people, preferably supportive friends. Depression often leads one to isolate themselves from others. Talking to someone every day is as beneficial as seeing a therapist. Social support and being part of a community has the greatest impact on health for people over the age of fifty than anything else. We are social creatures and were created to have relationships with other people.

Implement a schedule. This will ensure you give yourself enough time to sleep, eat, and take care of the basic necessities in your life. Budget time for eight hours of sleep, three meals a day, and schedule a time for the walk mentioned above or to exercise.

Eat three healthy meals a day. Your diet plays a huge role in overall health and your state of mind. Avoid excess sugar, which can cause a reduction of energy levels and increased mood swings.

Time: Most all depression goes away given time. The body is created to survive and respond as needed to keep us alive. Research has shown, for most, depressive symptoms will go away on their own in about the same amount of time for those who do nothing as opposed to those who take medication and see a therapist. If you have lost a parent, spouse, or child it may take one to two years to recover. It will get better, but sometimes it helps to know that it won't go on forever even when it feels like it will.

Entering a Broken System

Since the industrial revolution, men and women have been viewed increasingly as "consumers of resources" or assigned a numeric value based on productivity and career. Modern medicine and treatment philosophies in psychology have approached illness as if we are machines or at best animals. The goal is to look for what is broken and either repair or replace the faulty part. Behavioral psychology considers humans no more than animals to reward and control. Depression is a matter of reduced mood (chemistry) that impairs functioning. Obviously, the machine has to get back online so it can resume producing whatever it is supposed to produce. A pill is designed to improve mood, thus leading to an improvement in the ability to function. Prescribe the pill and observe the length of time until recovered. Therapy is generally problem focused and solution based for the short-term goal of returning the individual to functioning. It must be short-term and target a narrow range of behaviors because it is being paid for by a third party that is out to make a profit.

The insurance companies play the odds and restrict care certain times of the month or near the end of their fiscal year. Doctors and clinicians work the system to try and get the most days out of an insurance company or an increase in the number of sessions. The insurance companies won't approve sessions or treatment unless the problem is severe enough to require prescription medication. Physicians don't want angry patients who come with the expectation of getting a pill for quick recovery. They convince themselves what they are doing is the best for the patient, write prescriptions for two or three psychotropic medications, and move on to the next patient. They see so many patients they have forgotten who you are by the time you return in a month. Even with the notes from previous sessions, they don't really remember the deeper issues you had to really struggle to even speak about.

9

Understanding God and Myself

How does an understanding of God and spirituality help in my case?

Since the current approach to medicine and psychology does not take into consideration that man is a spiritual being, does that omission mean conventional treatment is inadequate? Men who didn't believe in God have heavily influenced the sciences. Their ideas and theories lead to most of the acceptable types of treatment used today. Some treatment providers are now approaching care more holistically because patients have demanded it, yet they don't know which way to go. Their whole approach is still based on theory that denies we are created beings or that we were created for a purpose. Think about that for a moment.

Depression is a response to something, but what? You can evaluate yourself and list a collection of symptoms, documenting their effect, but have difficulty pointing to something tangible that is depression. You might look at that depressed person and think, "they seem to carry a heavy load" or "appear overburdened." An individual's spirituality is only seen "out of our peripheral vision" so to speak, rather than looking at it straight on. A real relationship with God transforms a person to display the glory of God right in front of your eyes in a way that cannot be missed. If you are desperate to change and your current state of mind is depressed, perhaps you are now willing to "open the eyes" of your understanding.

But you don't know what I've been through...

Many of us have experienced some horrible things in our life. You may have come to think that if God were real then He wouldn't have let that happen to you. It is possible that something bad happened to you that was caused by someone who said they knew God or represented Him. When you're vulnerable and hurt you don't see that their actions are not anything like who Jesus was. These hurts or wounds try to define us our whole life. They get entrenched and then we've got our guard up against the church, against God, and against anyone who says they know Him. They say who we should trust and who we shouldn't trust. They tell us that we don't have any value because if we did, it wouldn't have happened. Either someone who was supposed to care for us would have stopped it from happening or God wouldn't have let it happen if He were real. We can use this event or series of events to cast blame the rest of our life. We can use it as justification to be mean and nasty, to drink or do drugs, or to avoid any sense of responsibility for the choices we make. We can become the wound and never see beyond it. This twisted perspective will keep someone depressed.

Sin entered the world because of man's disobedience.¹ God never intended for us to face the things we do. That's why He created a way out. His gift or provision is Jesus, His Son.² That was the price He was willing to pay so we could come back to Him like we were originally meant to walk, as in the garden. He is merciful and kind.³

My understanding and belief was full of hatred towards God for years over things I experienced as a child, then as a teen, and even more as an adult. I was such a wounded person, and I went around wounding others in my pain. I didn't even realize this was what I did because I was blinded by my own pain. I was so used to being in pain emotionally that I was numb so I didn't realize the full extent of it. I was hurt by people that were Christians. I thought if that was what God was like, I wanted no part of it. I kept everyone at arms' length, trusting nobody. I was so angry at the church and at God. I went searching for truth and began to study about religions of the world. I searched for a long time and wasn't satisfied with Buddhism, Islam, Hinduism, or any of the extra-Biblical spin-offs of Christianity (the groups that had an angel give them extra knowledge besides the Bible). I decided to approach the Bible the way I'd approached the books of the other faiths and simply read it. I found the people and churches around me were misrepresenting Christ by the way they expressed Him. Their message was contradicted through their lifestyles and choices. The Word of God itself was pure and beautiful. Jesus taught a way to live that blew me away. I began to consider, like the Word says, that my Father really did love me. I prayed and asked Him for a hug. I wanted to know what it felt like just once to experience a father's love and approval. He responded to me in a shocking way. I felt completely warmed and wrapped in a force and my whole body was flooded with joy for a few seconds. I stood there in shock, not quite believing it, but believing it at the same time.

God is love and He has revealed Himself through His Son, Jesus. Jesus took the punishment for our sins. He will take yours if you surrender to Him. He will heal all your wounds. Through Him we have been reconciled back to the Father.

Who You Really Are

Man was created in the image of God and for His purpose. We were created by Him to have an intimate relationship with Him. If you have never been told that or have never considered this truth, then you have never functioned as you were designed to function. The God of the universe who spoke creation into existence wants an intimate relationship with you because He loves you. We may have learned to move and operate in the physical realm with our senses and believed that is all there is. We may have functioned well, to some degree, and been happy some of the time, but this current depression says, "something is wrong." Even if your view of self and how you interact with the world is completely utilitarian, please consider this from the perspective of my assertion: Knowing and believing this will transform your understanding of who you are and you will begin to experience joy.[1]

God is our Father, we are His children. Without cultivating this relationship, we can never be whole in the way we were intended to be when created. It is impossible to grasp purpose without this relationship with our Father. Even if you have had an awareness of Him and called yourself a Christian, you may not understand this crucial part of your identity. When we function independently of our created purpose, over time there will be consequences and one of those is depression. Responding to this consequence with medication is like putting a band-aide over a wound in your soul. In understanding this idea, you have to consider that our Father made it possible for us to come close through Jesus Christ.[11]

Jesus Christ is the way the Father has provided for us to return to Him. We have been reconciled (brought near, restored in relationship) by the blood of Jesus. Since the way has been provided, the Father doesn't spare us simply because we want to go our own way. He is merciful and loves us. The only possible way to be restored to what our created value and purpose is comes through the cross of Jesus Christ.[12] We must believe on Him and what His work meant, repent of our sins, and be baptized. Ask to receive the Holy Spirit afterwards. This gives us freedom to come close to the Father.[13]

If you are an unbeliever, entering this relationship with your Father through Jesus will alleviate depression or depressive symptoms. It will set you free from yourself. If you are already a believer, then it is possible you don't know who you really are. When your identity is firmly fixed in Christ, depression becomes rare and is usually just a response to major life events. It is generally short-term if experienced at all because you are in regular fellowship with your Father and "count it all joy."[1]

I am not trying to sell you on the idea that "if you get saved you won't be depressed." I am not trying to entice you into a relationship with your Father by listing all the benefits from it, although there are benefits. Out of love, I am telling you the truth: You were created for relationship with your Father in heaven. He paid a very high price for you to be able to come near Him again. That price was His Son, Jesus' death on the cross to pay for our sins. The way and means for us to be transformed back into what we were originally intended to be has been provided. That is His mercy. No amount of anger or frustration or pride on your part will change that. If you are rejecting His provision, you are choosing death. When you are experiencing depression or the symptoms of depression and you have not had this relationship to your Father, it is your body and mind's response to not having what it needs. Even if you haven't known the truth of your created purpose, your body, mind, and spirit will cry out for that relationship with more frequency and disturbance until it is given some attention. A child requires the nurturing of its parent to be whole. Medications will only mask the pain and give false signals to the rest of your body. Even if you don't realize you are choosing death by rejecting the Son, as a created being your heart and flesh will demonstrate signs of this rejection.[1]

10

The Spiritual Roots of Depression

Depression often has the same roots for believers and unbelievers. If you have not yet been reconciled with your Father in heaven and cleansed by the blood of Christ to become righteous, this will not benefit you. You must submit to the authority of Jesus Christ as Lord in order to have the power to do the exercises and prayers below. It is by becoming sons and daughters that we receive the power and authority to break off strongholds and bondage.

Un-forgiveness

If we know the truth and have understood the forgiveness of our own sins by Christ, we must forgive others. If we make a choice not to forgive, no matter the offense, then we are choosing death. Think of the Lord's prayer: "forgive us our trespasses as we forgive those who have trespassed against us" (see Matthew 6:12). We will be forgiven according to the standard by which we forgive others. Jesus said that offense was a trap laid by Satan. It is the primary way in which the enemy gets us.

> **Then He said to the disciples, "It is impossible that no offenses should come, but woe to him through whom they do come!**
> **"It would be better for him if a millstone were hung around his neck, and he were thrown into the sea, than that he should offend one of these little ones.**
> **"Take heed to yourselves. If your brother sins against you, rebuke him; and if he repents, forgive him" (Luke 17:1-3 NKJV).**

We often have a "right" to be upset, hurt, or offended. Many of us have experienced horrendous offenses to ourselves or those we love. We certainly may perceive it as our "right" to hold people accountable or maintain that grievance. They are the ones who did wrong. Scripture clearly states that if we don't forgive those who have wronged us, then we forfeit our forgiveness of sins.

> "But if you do not forgive men their trespasses, neither will your Father forgive your trespasses" (Matthew 6:15 NKJV).

> "Therefore if you bring your gift to the altar, and there remember that your brother has something against you,
> "leave your gift there before the altar, and go your way. First be reconciled to your

brother, and then come and offer your gift" (Matthew 5:23-24 NKJV),

We are essentially damning ourselves by holding onto the sins of others. Jesus said if we didn't forgive others our Father would not forgive us. When we have experienced betrayal or hurt and do not forgive, we become bitter. This bitterness corrupts everything about us. We may not even recognize it and believe we've moved on. Often we run away from this pain. The bitterness brought about by refusing to forgive will cause depression.

You don't have to feel it to forgive. It is not about feeling, but about obedience. I have had difficulty forgiving some people in my life. I didn't really want to do it because the offense had been so great. Since my Father knows all about it anyway, I couldn't hide it and saw no need even as I prayed.

> *"Father, I forgive them for what they did to me. I don't feel like it or hardly even want to do it. I am forgiving because You said to do it and You forgave me. I want to do what You want me to do. I give up my right to be offended over what they have done. I forgive them and ask You to bless that person."*

You may have to pray this prayer multiple times. Any time you are reminded of the offense or how they hurt you and feel the feelings of anger associated with the event, pray for them and specifically tell your Father you forgive them and choose not to hold it against them. This will give you freedom from the bondage and bitterness. This will alleviate depression.

When Jesus says the most important commandment is: **"Love the Lord your God with all your heart, soul, and mind"** and **"You shall love your neighbor as yourself"** (see Matthew 22:37, 39), we often overlook the part about loving ourselves. It is important that we forgive ourselves for anything we've done and not hold our own sins against us. This is part of loving yourself that is essential to being able to love your neighbor. Think about the painful memory that still has the power to make you feel angry, hurt, or shame when it comes to mind. Pray the following:

> *"Father, I forgive myself for _____. I release any offense towards myself and ask You to heal this wound. I forgive anyone involved with my sin. I ask You, Holy Spirit, to seal up my heart from this wound and cut any tie creating a stronghold. I pray this in the name of Jesus, Amen.*

You don't have to be exact with this. You are just being honest with God who loves you completely and wants the best for you.

Unrepentant Sin

We can have sin in our life that we don't want to acknowledge or maybe even are pretending it is not sin. Sin will separate us from our Father and lead to distressing symptoms such as depression. The sin may be refusing to forgive someone like I mentioned above. When we feel the spiritual consequences of the separation from our Father it is our body, mind, and spirit cluing us in that there is a problem. He created us with every possible means for our survival. To remain in sin or reject that relationship is to condemn ourselves to hell.

Ask the Holy Spirit to show you any sin in your life. You

probably already know what it is even as you began reading this section. Some typical things people hold onto and justify that are sinful and separate one from God: relationships that violate covenant, pornography (involves lust, idolatry, coveting the wife of someone else), addictions, continuing to do something we know God has directed us to stop doing. Any of these things that we know separates us from the Father yet we continue to do is sin. Believers often don't recognize that the things they are viewing on television and the Internet are leading them to covet or desire what the Father has not chosen to give them.

There may be something we have done that we believe is unforgiveable. It may be some secret sin from our past that nobody even knows about. It has been planted like a land mine in our past by the enemy that is waiting to go off. We may have asked God for forgiveness, but know that sometimes we must ask forgiveness from the person we have wronged. This is dangerous territory for some people because you may have done something that if confessed could lead to jail or prison. It could lead to repercussions financially, relationally, and legally that could be life changing. If you have something like this ask the Holy Spirit to guide you and be obedient. Many Christians give counsel based on a psychological reason or based on what they believe will be best for you in the long run. This advice is based out of their own wisdom or experience. It often goes counter to the Word of God and is biased because they value your approval more than God's.

The Occult

A third category here that really falls under unrepentant sin is something many believers don't recognize. Current or past associations with the occult can lead to depression manifested in feelings of hopelessness or worthlessness. These have to be identified and repented of. In the book of Acts when people believed and were reconciled to their Heavenly Father, they knew they had to get rid of idols and books or trinkets that were associated with the occult.

> "Also, many of those who had practiced magic brought their books together and burned them in the sight of all. And they counted-up the value of them, and it totaled fifty thousand pieces of silver" (Acts 19:19 NKJV).

> "And have no fellowship with the unfruitful works of darkness, but rather expose them" (Ephesians 5:11 NKJV).

Ask Jesus to identify these things in your life if they are present. Rid your household of any associations with the occult and pray like this:

> *"Father, I renounce any association with the works of darkness. I renounce and give up any association or agreement I have made with demons. I renounce any vow or blood oath I have made either willfully or in ignorance. Forgive me for these relationships and cleanse me with the blood of Jesus. I ask Holy Spirit to seal my heart, mind, and soul where any of these wounds or memories were attached. Show me any wickedness that may be in me that I may confess it before You. Please reveal to me any object or item I should get rid of in my household that is an idol connected to the demonic. I ask this in the name of the Son, Jesus. Amen.*

Take the time to repent of each thing specifically that comes to mind. You may want to write them down if there are a lot. You are cutting the ties to these things by renouncing and repenting each association. Ask the Holy Spirit to seal your heart after each tie is cut.

Poor or False Perspective

This means we are not seeing our situation and circumstances in the right way. Perspective has everything to do with how we choose to interpret events daily. When we personalize any negative or poor treatment received and assign blame for the slightest fault, our perspective is twisted. If we are looking at the thing happening in the moment rather than seeing our whole life as a concentrated marathon, the loss in the short-term will wreck us. We will believe it reflects our value. If we consider that the life we have in its seventy to eighty-year span is all there is, then each misfortune or mistake is amplified. The death of a loved one is goodbye forever. Knowing Jesus takes away death's sting. When our loved ones die who also knew Him, we can be comforted by the knowledge that we will see them again. As believers, we can know that bearing the burden of everything is not something we have to do. We also know that through Jesus Christ, **"Yet in all these things we are more than conquerors through Him who loved us"** (Romans 8:37 NKJV).

If we live our lives from a right perspective, we will have the knowledge that this world is not our home. When we believe and were baptized:

> **Or do you not know that as many of us as were baptized into Christ Jesus were baptized into His death? Therefore, we were**

> buried with Him through baptism into death, that just as Christ was raised from the dead by the glory of the Father, even so we also should walk in newness of life (Romans 6:3-4 NKJV).

Our perspective is based out of newness of life. We can now come close to our Father and talk with Him as Jesus did. We can now have the Holy Spirit that gives power to overcome anything.

> But if the Spirit of Him who raised Jesus from the dead dwells in you, He who raised Christ from the dead will also give life to your mortal bodies through His Spirit who dwells in you (Romans 8:11 NKJV).

11

Know Who You Are and How To Fight

Your Identity and Weapons of Warfare

We may not know who we really are "in Christ." This identity crisis comes from not having a firm foundation of understanding who we are and what it means to be a Christian.

> "My people perish for lack of knowledge..." (Hosea 4:6).

If we don't have a firm grasp on our identity, we won't understand the consequences of wearing a uniform on a battlefield in the midst of the enemy, with no idea how to fight.

> Be sober, be vigilant; because your adversary the devil walks about like a roaring lion, seeking whom he may devour.

> **Resist him, steadfast in the faith, knowing that the same sufferings are experienced by your brotherhood in the world.**
> **But may the God of all grace, who called us to His eternal glory by Christ Jesus, after you have suffered a while, perfect, establish, strengthen, and settle you (I Peter 5:8-10 NKJV.)**

If you are a Christian, if you believe, you are in a battle whether you like it or not. Your identity and purpose matters a great deal. We face an enemy, Satan, who is our adversary. An adversary is someone who opposes us and is our enemy. He seeks to devour us. That means this enemy will try to consume us or destroy us. He is also called a thief: **"The thief does not come except to steal, and to kill, and to destroy. I have come that they may have life, and that they may have it more abundantly"** (John 10:10 NKJV).

He is a thief because he takes from us. This enemy will take all he can to the point of destroying us. He will take our peace, our confidence, our courage, our joy, and even our very identity. How, you may be asking, does he take even our identity? Jesus identified what the devil is like when talking to a Pharisee: **"You are of your father the devil, and the desires of your father you want to do. He was a murderer from the beginning, and does not stand in the truth, because there is no truth in him. When he speaks a lie, he speaks from his own resources, for he is a liar and the father of it"** (John 8:44 NKJV).

He is a liar and is constantly whispering in our ear that we are not who our Father has said we are. Satan points us to what we don't have rather than to what we do have. He accuses us of things from our past that we've already received forgiveness for. He convinces us to take things personally. He sows division among family members, brethren, and acquaintances. Satan is not everywhere like God. He is limited compared to our Heavenly Father and Jesus, but he does command a hierarchy of fallen angels and demons.

> **And the angels who did not keep their proper domain, but left their own abode, He has reserved in everlasting chains under darkness for the judgment of the great day (Jude 1:6 NKJV).**

> **Put on the whole armor of God, that you may be able to stand against the wiles of the devil.**
> **For we do not wrestle against flesh and blood, but against principalities, against powers, against the rulers of the darkness of this age, against spiritual hosts of wickedness in the heavenly places (Ephesians 6:11-12 NKJV).**

There are two words that clue us in on what we will be doing as believers—wrestling and standing. We are to resist the devil. The state of a Christian believer is that of a warrior in a battle. He is intended to be armored up and active in the fight. Many of us were taught to choose when to do this depending upon where we were going at any given time. Most of us don't have any concept of what a real battle would look like. Can you imagine being surrounded by forces fighting for their lives on an open field, then sitting down in the middle of it all, reading a book and having a cup of tea?

Be convinced of what your role is as a believer with the truth of God's Word. You have received knowledge that will help you avoid perishing with the people who don't have it. Get angry with the enemy—get angry with him for trying to steal from you, your family, and from your future. It is one thing to feel depressed, suffer the effects, and not know why you are experiencing this. It is quite another to know you are being targeted specifically because of who you are and who your Father is. Let that thought rise inside you and get angry with this enemy and all he has stolen from you.

You have been depressed. Reading these words might feel overwhelming and make you believe it is just heaping more responsibilities on you when you can't handle the ones you have now. You don't feel like fighting. The good news is that you know the truth. God is merciful. His grace works in a way that requires you to move first, and then you will have the power and ability to overcome this. You choose to move out of obedience and faith, and then you will receive what you need to overcome and conquer.

You don't get to sit out of this fight because of how you are feeling. You know the truth. Your only option out is to reject Christ, and that is no option because it leads to death. So, you must fight. We have labeled the enemy as a liar, a thief, a prowler, a devourer, and an accuser. His attacks come at us through our thoughts and through our minds. He will use others to attack us in the same way, by distorting thoughts and feelings as well as causing false beliefs. Where then, do we go to battle him?

> **I beseech you therefore, brethren, by the mercies of God, that you present your bodies a living sacrifice, holy, acceptable to God, which**

> is your reasonable service.
> And do not be conformed to this world, but be transformed by the renewing of your mind, that you may prove what is that good and acceptable and perfect will of God (Romans 12:1-2 NKJV).

Our reasonable service will come through our mind's renewal as we are being transformed. This transformation will take place by ingesting the truth and knowledge of who we really are and what it means to be a Christian. Listening to the enemy has filled my mind and spirit with thoughts or beliefs such as: "I am helpless, things are hopeless, I will never change, I will always be this way, nobody will ever really love me, I can't be saved, I'm not even a Christian, look at the way I've lived, I might as well give up, I am a failure and will never amount to anything." Can you relate to those messages playing in your head? Those are lies, they are garbage, and they need to be washed out of your spirit and mind. We wash them out and cleanse our mind with the Word of God. Read this Scripture and let the Holy Spirit apply it personally.

> Husbands, love your wives, just as Christ also loved the church and gave Himself for her,
> that He might sanctify and cleanse her with the washing of water by the word,
> that He might present her to Himself a glorious church, not having spot or wrinkle or any such thing, but that she should be holy and without blemish (Ephesians 5:25-27 NKJV).

"The church" in the above Scripture is you, me, and every other believer who is following Jesus. When we have those thoughts running in our head, we counter them with the Word of God. The stronghold is created by hearing a lie, believing it, and then acting on that agreement in our responses.

> For though we walk in the flesh, we do not war according to the flesh.
> For the weapons of our warfare are not carnal but mighty in God for pulling down strongholds,
> casting down arguments and every high thing that exalts itself against the knowledge of God, bringing every thought into captivity to the obedience of Christ,
> and being ready to punish all disobedience when your obedience is fulfilled (II Corinthians 10:3-6 NKJV).

The weapons we are given to fight this battle are "mighty in God" for pulling down strongholds. The strongholds were built in our mind and spirit when we believed the lies of the enemy over the truth of what our Father said about who we are. We did not know, in our ignorance, to cast down the devil's argument that we have no value or are worthless. We let it stand against the knowledge of God as if it were true!

> But God, who is rich in mercy, because of His great love with which He loved us,
> even when we were dead in trespasses, made us alive together with Christ (by grace you have been saved), and raised us up together, and made us sit together in the

> **heavenly places in Christ Jesus (Ephesians 2:4-6 NKJV).**

That doesn't sound like something that has no value or purpose, does it? How can I be unlovable if God, who created everything and set all of creation into motion, says His love for me is "great?" It says I am made to sit in the heavenly places with Jesus. The truth of God's Word counters any lie that I have no purpose.

> **Just as He chose us in Him before the foundation of the world, that we should be holy and without blame before Him in love (Ephesians. 1:4 NKJV.)**

I am not some random accidental person put here on this earth to simply exist. He chose me before the world was even made and loved me.

> **Behold what manner of love the Father has bestowed on us, that we should be called children of God! Therefore, the world does not know us, because it did not know Him (I John 3:1 NKJV).**

What is my identity according to Scripture? I am a child of God. My being called is an honor that demonstrates His love for me. If the world doesn't know the Father and respond accordingly, how can I expect it to know me and respond accordingly? Let's take time to counter some of the lies by proclaiming truth over ourselves. Pray something like this:

> *Father, I thank You that You chose me before the foundation of the world. I thank You that You*

chose me for holiness and have called me Your child. I know that You love me because it says so in Your Word. I thank You that Your love for me was so great You made me to sit with Jesus in the heavenly places. I take captive any lie of the enemy and cast it down. This word is truth. I pray this in the name of Your Son, Jesus Christ.

We are proclaiming truth of the Word of God over our lives and pulling down the stronghold of deceit. When you begin to pray this way, you will feel something shift around you in the spirit realm. You have struck a blow in battle against the destroyer and will begin to feel how mighty these weapons are.

12

The Past: Let It Go

Many believers are tormented by things that either happened to them in their past or things they did themselves. This connects to the principle of forgiveness and forgiving ourselves. Sometimes, to put something to rest, will take repeated prayer along with the "washing of the word."

> Brethren, I do not count myself to have apprehended; but one thing I do, forgetting those things which are behind and reaching forward to those things which are ahead,
> I press toward the goal for the prize of the upward call of God in Christ Jesus (Philippians. 3:13-14 NKJV.)

Paul, the guy who wrote the letter to the Philippian church, is saying he had not yet attained or apprehended the goal. He knew the power the past could have over someone. He participated in the murder of Stephen before he met Jesus. Keeping our mind on the things of the past leads to uncertainty about our current direction and goal.

> **Therefore, we also, since we are surrounded by so great a cloud of witnesses, let us lay aside every weight, and the sin which so easily ensnares us, and let us run with endurance the race that is set before us,**
> **looking unto Jesus, the author and finisher of our faith, who for the joy that was set before Him endured the cross, despising the shame, and has sat down at the right hand of the throne of God (Hebrews 12:1-2 NKJV).**

The things that are in our past are "dead works." To be completely accurate, they are the actions of the dead because we died with Christ and have been raised with Him. We are new creatures following belief, repentance, and baptism. The old acts or sins of the old man are no longer a part of who we are. We sometimes make the mistake of believing the words of "the accuser" when he reminds us of our past failures or sins. If he can get us to believe we are not forgiven and deceive us into taking on the shame or fear of consequences from that past deed, then we agree with his lies. If we agree, we are effectively saying the blood of Christ was not enough. Remember, it is not about feelings but about agreeing with truth whether you feel good or not. Sometimes things keep coming up in our mind as areas of torment because we need to seek reconciliation with a brother or sister in Christ.

> Therefore, if you bring your gift to the altar, and there remember that your brother has something against you, leave your gift there before the altar, and go your way. First be reconciled to your brother, and then come and offer your gift (Matthew 5:23-24 NKJV).

If there are questions about reconciliation, seek the counsel of a mature believer you trust, but remember the flesh always wants to take the easy way out. Ask the Holy Spirit to direct you and continue to put it on your mind if you are to reconcile. If you have harmed another brother or sister, you may feel growth and progress has stopped until you ask their forgiveness. This can be one of the hardest things you ever do, but it is worth it in the long run. We are required and it is part of not becoming a stumbling block to another.

13

The Potential Pitfall and Problems of Therapy and Treatment

Therefore, since we are the offspring of God, we ought not to think that the Divine Nature is like gold or silver or stone, something shaped by art and man's devising (Acts 17:29 NKJV).

There is no substitute for our intended relationship with the Father who created us in His image for His purpose. Without that relationship being mended, we will always feel "broken." We've been like orphans, not knowing our identity and wandering, believing nobody loved us or thought we had value. Healing will not come through the work of men's hands or their minds, but only through the words of our Father who spoke life into us through His Son, Jesus Christ. Speak the truth of God about who you are. Be shaped by the love of your Father.

The Potential Pitfall and Problems of Therapy and Treatment

Therapy and a diagnosis of Major Depressive Disorder can reinforce the deception of this world and allow you to feel it is ok to remain in your sin or disobedience. You may begin to take medication that could cloud your mind for years to come and numb the spiritual man or woman inside you. It gives you permission to be "sick" because it is an illness; therefore, you have an excuse to not address many things in your life and put them off as a result. Depression should make a person so miserable that they won't have any choice but to determine what is wrong and try to fix it. It can veil the truth and prohibit you from having eyes to see or ears to hear.

Remember, you are in a battle whether you choose to fight or not. The enemy is out to kill you and take everything you have. He does not fight fair. This truth may be hard to hold onto as all conventional "wisdom" in the world around you runs counter to understanding—YOU NEED THIS INTIMACY WITH GOD TO BE WHOLE AND FREE.

Countering the Lies

The Holy Bible is your history and God's message for you. It is meant to inform you about who you are. Since these words come from your Father in heaven, say the following aloud, knowing it is what the Father says about you and about me. If you can, I want you to go and stand in front of a mirror and look yourself in the eyes when you say these verses. Do this every day reciting at least one or two verses. As you can, increase to saying all these verses. It may take some time, but if you do this, you will have a moment when you see yourself through the eyes of your Heavenly Father. You will see you and have compassion, feel mercy, and understand that the Father loves you. Do this for as long as you need to transform your mind and spirit. Below each verse, I am going to paraphrase the content for your statement and make it personal. Say the paraphrased statement when you look yourself in the eye in a mirror.

> **Therefore, if the Son makes you free, you shall be free indeed (John 8:36 NKJV).**
> Say: *Jesus has made you free and you are truly free!*

> **For by grace you have been saved through faith, and that not of yourselves; it is the gift of God (Ephesians 2:8 NKJV).**
> Say: *You are saved. You don't have to earn it; it is a gift.*

> **For you did not receive the spirit of bondage again to fear, but you received the Spirit of adoption by whom we cry out, "Abba, Father." The Spirit Himself bears witness with our spirit that we are children of God (Romans 8:15-16 NKJV).**
> Say: *You have nothing to fear. You are adopted by Abba, Father and are His child. You have received His Spirit.*

> **He has delivered us from the power of darkness and conveyed us into the kingdom of the Son of His love,**
> **in whom we have redemption through His blood, the forgiveness of sins (Colossians 1:13-14 NKJV).**
> Say: *You are no longer under the power of*

darkness. You belong to the kingdom of God. You are redeemed through His blood and your sins are forgiven.

If we confess our sins, He is faithful and just to forgive our sins and to cleanse us from all unrighteousness (I John 1:9 NKJV.)
Say: *I am clean and pure. I am forgiven for all my sins. I am righteous.*

I will include more verses to speak aloud over yourself in a brief Appendix at the end of the book. These verses are sharp as swords. They are your weapons against the lying accuser. Say these out loud over yourself, understanding that it is the Word of God who created you speaking these words. It is in hearing this Word and accepting it is for you and about you that pulls down the strongholds in your mind and transforms you into the man or woman of God you were meant to be. This is the battle and it is for your mind. This is putting on the armor of God by building your shield of faith, by "hearing of the Word."

14

Make Your List: Divine Cognitive Therapy

If any of the science or research based techniques created by man work, it is because they have discovered some part of truth that God has made evident in creation already. An example of this is one of the most frequently used therapy techniques, Cognitive Behavioral Therapy. There used to be a comedy skit on *Saturday Night Live* where a character would look into a mirror and say to himself—"I'm good enough, I'm smart enough, and doggone it, people like me." He was poking fun at a technique to use positive affirmations in countering negative thoughts. It is based on an idea that continually hearing positive statements about ourselves will eventually lead to our believing it.

To get more technical and into the therapeutic lingo it is called thought replacement. You will take a few days to monitor or record the irrational, negative, or harmful thoughts that bring on feelings of worthlessness. You can also just write them down if you have a good memory. Once you've written down all the negative thoughts that left you feeling down for a few days, you examine each one for truth, exaggeration, and whether it is rational. CBT (Cognitive Behavioral Therapy) has been considered the most used and effective technique for addressing certain therapeutic issues such as low self-esteem that accompany depression. The difficulty comes in believing what you are saying about yourself. It requires having worked through the reason your negative thoughts are not true, thus proving they are irrational. Much of the choice for believing positive affirmations about oneself is based on how much credibility or authority we give the one who is making the statements.

There is no higher authority than our Father in heaven. Acknowledge Him as your Creator and understand the right He has to proclaim who you are over your life. His Word in Scripture is what we will use for our affirmations as we began to list in the previous chapter. Man's wisdom, psychology, might label these negative statements your "script" and suggest it is coming from your own mind. That is not true. These negative self-statements are not "self-statements," they are the voice of our enemy, the one who wants to steal, kill, and destroy us. When you make a list of all the negative things that you hear in your mind about yourself, then you are supposed to counter those things with a positive statement. What I am going to ask you to do is first pray the prayer below, then make a list of things you sometimes think about that lead to feelings of frustration, sadness, hopelessness, or grief about yourself.

A Prayer

Father, I cry out to You. I need You. I need help. I believe in Jesus, Your Son, that He took the punishment for my sin. I believe that He bled on the cross for me and died. Because He did what He did, I am free. I am no longer bound by sin or death. There is no condemnation for me. I apply that blood to my life, my mind, and everything about who I am. I am cleansed from all unrighteousness. I have been called a (son or daughter) by Him. Search me and reveal each lie of the enemy that I have come into agreement with. I break this agreement and rebuke any curse upon my life that was placed through believing a lie or that someone else has spoken over me. Holy Spirit, I yield to Your work in me. Write the word upon my heart that the strongholds of the enemy are torn down. I pray this, Father, in the name of Your Son Jesus. Amen.

For this is the covenant that I will make with the house of Israel after those days, says the LORD: I will put My laws in their mind and write them on their hearts; and I will be their God, and they shall be My people (Hebrews 8:10 NKJV).

Making the List: (Write, leaving a line or two between each statement.)

Think of the things that you believe about yourself that you don't like or that cause you pain. These may be words you remember someone said about you that hurt. They may have been said by a parent, a girlfriend, a boyfriend, a friend, a spouse, or a sibling. Now you repeat those statements to yourself. It might look something like this:

- I always mess things up (jobs, relationships, finances).
- I will never be good enough or be successful.
- Nobody truly loves me. I am unlovable.
- I am a failure.
- I am stupid.
- I am a loser.
- I am ugly.
- I am fat.
- Even your own parents didn't want you.
- I hate myself.
- I am worthless. I have no value.
- I am evil and cannot be saved.
- I will never be anything more than I am now.

Everyone's list will be different. You may not have any of these negative things spoken by the enemy coming at you. Yours could take the shape of repeatedly being led astray from one thing to another. We will counter these lies of the enemy with the Word of God to pull down any strongholds the enemy has built in your mind to steal from you. I will provide you with Scriptural truths about all believers that you will begin to speak aloud over your own life. When we speak these truths aloud, we are agreeing with our Father in heaven and proclaiming our identity to the principalities and powers. The Scriptures will be in the Appendix section at the end of the book.

15

Depression In the Bible

The Bible's Take on Depression

There are several people mentioned in the Bible that appeared to be what we might call depressed. Our concept of depression is a false one that doesn't take into account the goals or agenda behind those who determined that a label needed to be given for that specific set of symptoms. Taking that into consideration, we can still go to Scripture and get insight into situations that led to melancholy or sadness on the part of the individual. Beginning with the Old Testament, here is an account of who demonstrated prolonged sadness and what was going on in their life.

Job: Job is perhaps the best-known person in the Bible who had every type of bad thing happen in his life. Job was sifted by the enemy and lost his wife, children, and all his property. He expressed feelings of despair but never gave up and cursed God. His wife urged him to curse God before she died. His friends badgered him to discover how he had sinned to deserve what was happening to him.

Elijah: Following his big three-year struggle and showdown where he killed the prophets of Baal and called fire down from heaven, he ran for his life. He made statements that indicated he felt he was all alone. He talked to God about everyone like him being dead but God said He preserved a remnant. He went to hide out in a cave and feared for his life that Jezebel was going to kill him. He asked God to let him die (see I Kings 19:4-5). This was a faithful servant of God, a prophet who walked with God enough to be able to call fire down from heaven and ask God to hold the rain for three years and it didn't rain. After all this he is worn out physically, lonely, and wishing to die.

David: David had some difficult times when Saul was trying to kill him and he had to run and fight all the time. He didn't appear to be depressed though, until he sinned by taking Bathsheba from Uriah. When he was confronted by his sin of lust, adultery, and murder, David fell apart. His Psalms of lament were indicative of depression. He begged the Lord to take his life at times and also begged that the Lord wouldn't take away His Holy Spirit. He was also "greatly distressed" when his wife was taken away in captivity. Psalm 102 is definitely about depression. The story of David illustrates how depression comes often with sin and its consequences. David's depression was lifted when he repented and cried out to the Lord. He still had physical consequences in his life from his sin of adultery, but overcame the depression.

Jonah: He was angry about being told by God to go to Nineveh. He was prejudiced against those God was telling him to warn. Jonah had obvious anger in his heart towards these people. Jonah was disobedient and then tried to hide from his relationship with God. He tried to run even though he knew it was wrong and was swallowed by a whale. He left the support of others and cut off contact with God because he was sinning in his disobedience. There were drastic consequences for Jonah's disobedience and he cried out, **"The waters surrounded me, even to my soul; the deep closed around me; weeds were wrapped around my head. I went down to the moorings of the mountains; the earth with its bars closed behind me forever; yet You have brought up my life from the pit, O LORD, my God"** (Jonah 2:5-6 NKJV). He was stuck in "the fat" of the whale until it spit him out. After all of that he gave in and did what God asked of him. He preached to the Ninevites but became angry that they listened and repented. He was so upset they had listened and been spared that he expressed, **"Therefore now, O LORD, please take my life from me, for it is better for me to die than to live!"** (Jonah 4:3 NKJV) Jonah felt those people did not deserve to be spared because they were so awful.

Peter: He was full of zeal and desire to serve Jesus and would not have believed he'd have ended up where he did. Jesus told Peter he would deny Him three times, but Peter didn't believe it. When Jesus had been taken and all the disciples scattered in fear, Peter was asked if he'd known Him. **Peter said, "Man, I do not know what you are saying!" Immediately, while he was still speaking, the rooster crowed. And the Lord turned and looked at Peter. And Peter remembered the word of the Lord, how He had said to him, "Before the rooster crows, you will deny Me three times." So Peter went out and wept bitterly"** (Luke 22:60-62 NKJV). Peter experienced depression or sorrow and regret for what he'd done. He "wept bitterly." He later received forgiveness from Jesus when He was resurrected. He repented of his denial and reconciled their relationship.

Judas: There is not much to say about him other than he was obviously depressed because of his betrayal of Christ. He could have repented like Peter did, but instead chose to take his own life by hanging.

Paul: Paul reported feeling overwhelmed and depressed. He says, "we despaired of life itself" in II Corinthians 1:8. In verses 9-10, Paul speaks of **"Yes, we had the sentence of death in ourselves, that we should not trust in ourselves but in God who raises the dead, who delivers us from so great a death, and does deliver us; in whom we trust that He will still deliver us."** Paul refers to their party as "downcast" in II Corinthians 7:5-6. **"For indeed, when we came to Macedonia, our bodies had no rest, but we were troubled on every side. Outside were conflicts, inside were fears. Nevertheless God, who comforts the downcast, comforted us by the coming of Titus."** Here you see his expression of being uplifted by his contact with his friend Titus. Paul is burdened by concern for others in the churches he has planted, his life is constantly being threatened, he is being lied about by people he thought were fellow ministers, and he is beaten and imprisoned regularly. He is comforted by the closeness of his relationship with his Father whom he walks with in intimacy. Because of this relationship, he is able to rejoice and sing praises even when in the midst of the worst tribulation. Paul distinguishes between kinds of sorrow in the following verse:

For godly sorrow produces repentance

> leading to salvation, not to be regretted; but the sorrow of the world produces death.
>
> For observe this very thing, that you sorrowed in a godly manner: What diligence it produced in you, what clearing of yourselves, what indignation, what fear, what vehement desire, what zeal, what vindication! In all things you proved yourselves to be clear in this matter (II Corinthians 7:10-11).

Their sorrow led to repentance, which "cleared" them. We were created for relationship with our Father and without that being in right and good standing, we will be miserable. The misery gets worse the longer we go without responding to Him. Many have not known this is what they are missing.

16

Fear and Loneliness

Are You Afraid?

Something to point out here is an obvious characteristic in each of these biblical stories. Every one of these people was experiencing fear along with everything else they had to deal with. The fear followed disobedience to God and sin in each case, except for Paul's. David was fearful the Lord would take away the Holy Spirit from him and he could no longer know God. Jonah was afraid because he'd been disobedient and knew why everything was happening in his life. It is a healthy thing to fear the Lord and being separated from Him. This is particularly true if we have sin or disobedience in our life.

> **We have not received a spirit of fear leading to slavery again but have received a**

> spirit of adoption as sons by which we cry out, Abba Father (Romans 8:15 NKJV).

Fear is the opposite of faith and results from a spirit. We actually have the authority to command it leave as believers. Many people diagnosed with depression report trouble with anxiety that interferes with their day-to-day activities. Anxiety can go hand-in-hand with depression and is an irrational fear with no basis in reality. The antidote for anxiety is to push in to the Father, realize who you are in Christ, and choose to die to yourself. Anxiety will often contribute to sleepless nights. In Paul's second letter to Timothy he says:

> For God has not given us a spirit of fear, but of power and of love and of a sound mind (II Timothy 1:7).

This leads to what we are promised when we believe and are baptized. Jesus said He would send the Comforter, the Holy Spirit, who would guide us into all truth. Without this relationship with your Father through Jesus the Son, you don't have the Holy Spirit. This is the Spirit of Power that will indwell us and make it possible to live a holy life. If you are a believer and doubt you have this, ask now for your Father in heaven to give you the Holy Spirit. Many people are never taught by their tradition they should ask for the filling of the Holy Spirit and what it will mean for their walk.

Are You Lonely?

The scientific perspective even says "social support" is one of the biggest predictors of good health in older people. The more "alone" someone feels, the greater the weight of their problems. There is some truth to that for all ages. Look at the impact of loneliness on Jonah and Elijah.

We are meant to exist as believers in a body as an organism. We are interdependent and need to be around others who believe like we do. God created us this way. He means for us to walk with Him in fellowship and intimacy as well as walk with one another. When we are told by well-meaning people that we should go to church, it is often separated from the meaning of why we should, but there is good reason. Our Father, who created us and knows what we need most, said we should be together with other believers and remind each other who we are. Encourage one another in the midst of this battle we are in that we realized when we first began reading this book.

> **And let us consider one another in order to stir up love and good works, not forsaking the assembling of ourselves together, as is the manner of some, but exhorting one another and so much the more as you see the day approaching (Hebrews 10:25 NKJV.)**

It is essential you walk this walk with other people. I don't care how much of a loner you are, everyone needs companionship. The disciples were sent out at least in groups of two. It was important for them to remind one another where they came from and who they were. That is why it is essential to have other believers in your life regularly. The Word says:

> **Brethren, if a man is overtaken in any trespass, you who are spiritual restore such a one in a spirit of gentleness, considering**

> yourself lest you also be tempted. Bear one another's burdens, and so fulfill the law of Christ (Galatians 6:1-2 NKJV).

If you or I stumble and fall, we are close enough to one another to see it happen. We can help pick each other up and provide encouragement. I can confess the sin that leads me to stumble to my brother and receive prayer. It may be my awful family that frustrates me to the point of sin in the way that I treat others. When we are alone and away from others, we are easy game for the "roaring lion seeking whom he may devour."

> Is anyone among you sick? Let him call for the elders of the church, and let them pray over him, anointing him with oil in the name of the Lord.
> And the prayer of faith will save the sick, and the Lord will raise him up. And if he has committed sins, he will be forgiven.
> Confess your trespasses to one another, and pray for one another, that you may be healed. The effective, fervent prayer of a righteous man avails much.
> Elijah was a man with a nature like ours, and he prayed earnestly that it would not rain; and it did not rain on the land for three years and six months.
> And he prayed again, and the heaven gave rain, and the earth produced its fruit.
> Brethren, if anyone among you wanders from the truth, and someone turns him back,
> let him know that he who turns a sinner from the error of his way will save a soul from

death *and cover a multitude of sins (James 5: 14-20 NKJV).*

Pray this prayer:

> *Father, I believe You when You say in Your word "I will never leave you nor forsake you." I believe that there is nowhere I can go to be separated from Your love. I admit that You must love me because You paid a high price for me and said I was worth the blood of Your Son, Jesus. I accept the blood for my life and apply it as a priest would. I have been bought with the blood and belong to You. Restore me, Father, and give me Your Holy Spirit that has been promised. I command a spirit of fear, death, despair, and loneliness to leave me now in the name of Jesus and never return. Father, I ask You to seal my heart with Your Holy Spirit. Thank You in the name of Jesus. Amen.*

17

The Wrap Up

This is not the quick fix type of thing, although it will be for some. This is the surgery where you are transformed into a new creation. Christians may get depressed and the way out is the same. I guarantee that the more time you spend with your Father, the more joy you will experience. That means to forgive anyone you hold a grudge or resentment against. Repent of any sin you have in your life and turn away from it. Renounce the things of darkness and any occult associations you may have. End any illicit relationship you have that is adulterous or fornicating. Get baptized if you have not been for the remission of your sins. Ask for the Holy Spirit to inhabit you and fill you. He whom the Son sets free is free indeed.

I hope you have stayed with me throughout the pages and somewhere along the way have decided you need to renew your relationship with your Heavenly Father. If you ask Him to help you and want to explore this, He will. Sometime that is all we can manage. It is hard to trust if you've never experienced the love of a father or love from a Christian who convinced you this stuff is real. Please, take some of my faith today and believe, if just a little bit, that I was once profoundly depressed and thought life was over. I was restored by doing the very thing I am asking you to do. I was restored through my calling out to Him and risking beginning a relationship with my Father. I got to know Him by knowing Jesus. Ask Him to make Himself known to you. Think of the most real Christian you know or have met in your life, and seek them out. Ask them to pray with you.

If you don't have anyone to pray with now, you can pray on your own. Here's the prayer again from the front of the book just like I said. It is not about your saying the right thing. This is about you returning to your Father who loves you more than you'll ever know.

Pray the following prayer aloud before continuing. It is an important part of this process:

> *Father, I believe You sent Jesus to die for my sins. I believe and accept His sacrifice for me and know His shed blood cleanses me from all unrighteousness. I repent of my sins and give up my life. I apply the blood of Jesus to my past, my present, and my future. I am made whole and healed by Your work on the cross, Jesus. I renounce a spirit of death and despair in the name of Jesus. Father, please give me Your Holy Spirit and teach me about who I am and what my purpose is. Thank You and I love You. Amen.*

You will need other believers to fellowship with. Ask your Father to guide you somewhere. Think about the person you know that most represents Christ or who a Christian is and go where they go. Make sure what they teach and preach aligns with the Bible. If you haven't been baptized, you need to get that done. Be blessed and full of joy.

Appendix A—Scripture Verses Cited

Chapter 10 Scripture References:

1. Romans 5:12: **Therefore, just as through one man sin entered the world, and death through sin, and thus death spread to all men, because all sinned** (see Romans 5:13-21).

2. I John 2:2: **And He Himself is the propitiation for our sins, and not for ours only but also for the whole world.** (see also John 1:29)

3. Psalm 103:8: **The Lord is merciful and gracious, slow to anger, and abounding in mercy.**

4. II Timothy 3:5: **having a form of godliness but denying its power. And from such people turn away!**

5. Psalms 68:5 **A father of the fatherless, a defender of widows, Is God in His holy habitation.**

6. I John 4:8: **He who does not love does not know God, for God is love.**

7. II Corinthians 5:18: **Now all things are of God, who has reconciled us to himself through Jesus Christ, and has given us the ministry of reconciliation**

8. Genesis 1:26: **Then God said, "Let Us make man in Our image, according to Our likeness; let them have dominion over the fish of the sea, over the birds of the air, and over the cattle, over all the earth and over every creeping thing that creeps on the earth.**

9. <u>Hebrews 10:22</u>: **Let us draw near with a true heart in full assurance of faith, having our hearts sprinkled from an evil conscience and our bodies washed with pure water.**

10. <u>I Peter 1:6-8:</u> **In this you greatly rejoice, though now for a little while, if need be, you have been grieved by various trials, that the genuineness of your faith, being much more precious than gold that perishes, though it is tested by fire, may be found to praise, honor, and glory at the revelation of Jesus Christ, whom having not seen you love. Though now you do not see Him, yet believing, you rejoice with joy inexpressible and full of glory,**

    <u>II Corinthians 5:17</u>: **Therefore if anyone is in Christ, he is a new creation; old things have passed away; behold, all things have become new.**

    <u>I John 5:4</u>: **For whatever is born of God overcomes the world. And this is the victory that has overcome the world—our faith.**

11. <u>I Corinthians 1:18</u>: **For the message of the cross is foolishness to those who are perishing, but to us who are being saved it is the power of God.**

12. <u>Acts 2:38</u>: **Then Peter said to them, "Repent, and let every one of you be baptized in the name of Jesus Christ for the remission of sins; and you shall receive the gift of the Holy Spirit."**

    <u>Acts 3:19</u>: **Repent therefore and be converted, that your sins may be blotted out, so that times of refreshing may come from the presence of the Lord.**

13. <u>Galatians 5:1</u>: **Stand fast therefore in the liberty**

by which Christ has made us free, and do not be entangled again with a yoke of bondage.

Romans 8:15: For you did not receive the spirit of bondage again to fear, but you received the Spirit of adoption by whom we cry out, "Abba, Father."

I Peter 1:8-9: Whom having not seen you love. Though now you do not see Him, yet believing, you rejoice with joy inexpressible and full of glory, receiving the end of your faith—the salvation of your souls.

14. John 3:36: "He who believes in the Son has everlasting life; and he who does not believe the Son shall not see life, but the wrath of God abides on him."

John 1:12: But as many as received Him, to them He gave the right to become children of God, to those who believe in his name:

15. Psalm 84:2: My soul longs, yes, even faints for the courts of the Lord; My heart and flesh cry out for the living God.

Isaiah 26:9: With my soul I have desired You in the night, Yes, by my spirit within me I will seek You early; For when Your judgments are in the earth, the inhabitants of the world will learn righteousness.

Psalm 42:1-3: As the deer pants for the water brooks, so pants my soul for You, O God. My soul thirsts for God, for the living God. When shall I come and appear before God? My tears have been my food day and night, while they continually say to me, "Where is your God?"

Romans 8:19-22: **For the earnest expectation of the creation eagerly waits for the revealing of the sons of God. For the creation was subjected to futility, not willingly, but because of Him who subjected it in hope; because the creation itself also will be delivered from the bondage of corruption into the glorious liberty of the children of God. For we know that the whole creation groans and labors with birth pangs together until now.**

Appendix B

The following verses are to build your faith and are meant by our Father to teach us who we are in His kingdom. These verses are some of what your Father says about you. They will transform you by renewing your mind. Think and meditate on these things. Say them aloud in front of a mirror whenever possible. Substitute your own name for the pronouns to make it personal because it is.

I am a child of God and I believe in Him. "But as many as received Him, to them He gave the right to become children of God, to those who believe in His name" (John 1:12).

I have been adopted as a son (or daughter) because my Father really, really loves me and wanted to. "Having predestined us to adoption as sons by Jesus Christ to Himself, according to the good pleasure of His will" (Ephesians 1:5).

Jesus wants me to come to Him and He has accepted me. It is for God's glory. "Therefore receive one another, just as Christ also received us, to the glory of God" (Romans 15:7).

I am complete (as a believer) in Him. I know it is true because He is the head of all principality and powers. "And you are complete in Him, who is the head of all principality and power" (Colossians 2:10).

I am connected to Jesus. I have the same spirit as Jesus and am one with Him. "But he who is joined to the Lord is one spirit with Him" (I Corinthians 6:17).

I am a new creation. My past wrongs and sins died with Christ and have been done away with. I am free. "Knowing this, that our old man was crucified with Him, that the body of sin might be done away with, that we should no longer be slaves of sin" (Romans 6:6).

I am created in the image of God and He loves me. I have a purpose in life. "So God created man in His own image; in the image of God He created Him; male and female He created them" (Genesis 1:27).

My Father knew me before I was even born and loved me. "Before I formed you in the womb I knew you; before you were born I sanctified you; I ordained you a prophet to the nations" (Jeremiah 1:5).

I am a part of the body of Christ. I belong to Him. "Now you are the body of Christ, and members individually" (I Corinthians 12:27).

I have been chosen by God. I am special to Him. I have been called out of darkness and into His light. "But you are a chosen generation, a royal priesthood, a holy nation, His own special people, that you may proclaim the praises of Him who called you out of darkness into His marvelous light" (I Peter 2:9).

I have been baptized into Christ Jesus. I am one in Him with other believers. "For as many of you as were baptized into Christ have put on Christ. There is neither Jew nor Greek, there is neither slave nor free, there is neither male nor female; for you are all one in Christ Jesus" (Galatians 3:27-28).

I am not my own. My body is the temple of the Holy Spirit who is a gift from God. It matters greatly what I do with and to my body. "Or do you not know that your body is the temple of the Holy Spirit who is in you, whom you have from God, and you are not your own? (I Corinthians 6:19)

I am God's child. I will be like Him. This world will feel uncomfortable to me because it did to Him. "Behold what manner of love the Father has bestowed on us, that we should be called children of God! Therefore the world does not know us, because it did not know Him. Beloved, now we are children of God; and it has not been revealed what we shall be, but we know that when He is revealed, we shall be like Him, for we shall see Him as He is" (I John 3:1-2).

I have been lifted up, raised, to where Christ is. I am sitting with Him at God's right hand. My life is hidden in Him and I am completely safe. "If then you were raised with Christ, seek those things which are above, where Christ is, sitting at the right hand of God. Set your mind on things above, not on things on earth. For you died, and your life is hidden with Christ in God" (Colossians 3:1-3).

For additional resources on what the Father says about us visit: www.rolandholcombe.net

Abstract

Holsinger T., Steffens DC, Phillips C, Helms MJ, Breitner JC, Guralnik JM. "Head injury in early adulthood and the lifetime risk of depression". Arch Gen Psychiatry. January 2002

Jorgensen TS, Wium-Anderson IK, Wium-Anderson MK, Jorgensen MB. "Incidence of Depression After Stroke, and Associated Risk Factors and Mortality Outcomes, in a Large Cohort of Danish Patients." Journal of the American Medical Association—Psychiatry. October 1, 2016.

American Psychiatric Association. (2013). Diagnostic and statistical manual of mental disorders (5th ed.).Arlington, VA: American Psychiatric Publishing. Text citation:(American Psychiatric Association, 2013). http://dx.doi.org/10.1176/appi.books.9780890425596.dsm04

Notes

www.ingramcontent.com/pod-product-compliance
Lightning Source LLC
Chambersburg PA
CBHW031454040426
42444CB00007B/1098